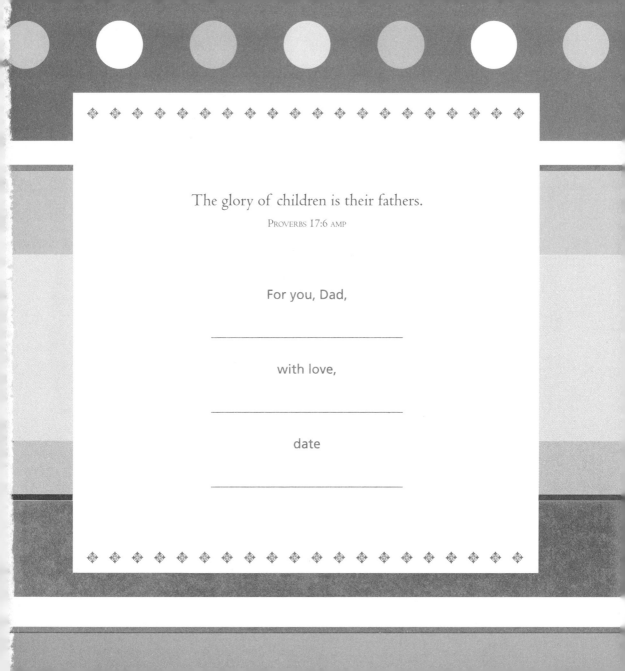

The glory of children is their fathers.

PROVERBS 17:6 AMP

For you, Dad,

_____

with love,

_____

date

_____

No music is so pleasant to my ears

as that word—*father.*

LYDIA MARIA CHILD

The
BEST
DAD
in the WORLD

HOWARD BOOKS
A DIVISION OF SIMON & SCHUSTER
New York   London   Toronto   Sydney

Our purpose at Howard Books is to:
- *Increase faith* in the hearts of growing Christians
- *Inspire holiness* in the lives of believers
- *Instill hope* in the hearts of struggling people everywhere
  Because He's coming again!

Published by Howard Books, a division of Simon & Schuster, Inc.
1230 Avenue of the Americas, New York, NY 10020
www.howardpublishing.com

The Best Dad in the World © 2008 by Dave Bordon & Associates, LLC

ISBN-13: 978-1-4165-5650-3
ISBN-10: 1-4165-5650-8

10 9 8 7 6 5 4 3 2 1

HOWARD and colophon are registered trademarks of Simon & Schuster, Inc.

Manufactured in the United States of America

For information regarding special discounts for bulk purchases, please contact: Simon & Schuster Special Sales at 1-800-456-6798 or business@simonandschuster.com.

Project developed by Bordon Books, Tulsa, Oklahoma
Project writing and compilation by Shawna McMurry and Christy Phillippe in association with Bordon Books
Edited by Chrys Howard
Cover design by Lori Jackson, LJ Design

Unless otherwise indicated, all Scripture quotations are taken from the *Holy Bible, New International Version®*. NIV®. Copyright © 1973, 1978, 1984 by International Bible Society. Used by permission of Zondervan. All rights reserved.

Scripture quotations marked NLT are taken from the *Holy Bible, New Living Translation,* copyright © 1996. Used by permission of Tyndale House Publishers, Inc., Wheaton, Illinois 60189. All rights reserved.

Scripture quotations marked AMP are taken from the *Amplified ® Bible,* copyright © 1954, 1958, 1962, 1964, 1965, 1987 by the Lockman Foundation. Used by permission. (www.Lockman.org)

Every effort has been made to obtain and provide proper and accurate source attributions for selections in this volume. If any attribution is incorrect, the publisher welcomes written documentation supporting correction for subsequent printings.

CONTENTS

What do I owe my father?

Everything.

HENRY VAN DYKE

INTRODUCTION

One of the most precious gifts given on this earth is a good father. A father who loves you and protects you. A father who accepts you just the way you are and yet challenges you to excel more. He is the first and most lasting impression in your life of what God the Father is like.

The Best Dad in the World celebrates the important role of fatherhood—but most especially, it honors *you,* my special dad, the one whom I've always looked up to. When I consider who you are and how you have lived your life, I am inspired to be the best I can be! I'm so glad God placed me in your life—and you in mine.

Dad, you're the best!

BEST
DAD
in the World Because...

You Love Me

Unconditionally.

There is no friendship, no love,

like that of the parent for the child.

HENRY WARD BEECHER

How great is the love the Father has lavished on us,
that we should be called children of God!

1 JOHN 3:1

Do you remember how you felt the first time you held your newborn baby? You were likely filled with wonder at the marvel of this tiny creation. Maybe you were nervous to hold someone who seemed so fragile, overwhelmed by the responsibility of it all. Did you imagine what the coming years might bring—reading bedtime stories, playing T-ball together, helping coach his football team, giving her away at her wedding? You undoubtedly felt a love beyond measure, a feeling that there is nothing you wouldn't do to care for this precious child. And that love only deepens with each passing year.

If you ever begin to doubt God's love for you, consider the love you have for your own children. There is nothing that could ever stop Him from loving you or that could cause Him to love you any less. You are His son, His treasured one.

A LETTER TO MY DAD

Dear Dad,

There's never been any doubt in my mind about whether you love me. I've made plenty of mistakes, and I know I've disappointed you at times, yet you've always made it clear that your love isn't based on my performance. Even when you've had to discipline me, you've shown your love by taking the time to talk to me and work with me toward a solution.

You've never let your pride get in the way of saying "I love you" often and with sincerity. You express your love in your words, your actions, and the time and attention you give to everyone in the family. Thank you for teaching me about God's love and about how to love other people through your unconditional love for me.

Love,

Your Child

Of all nature's gifts

to the human race,

what is sweeter to a man

than his children?

MARCUS TULLIUS CICERO

WHY I'M THANKFUL
YOU'RE MY DAD . . .

. . . You always gave the best

piggyback rides!

DANCING WITH DADDY

PAULA J. MILLER

My first memory of him was at their wedding. I don't recall the sun shining through the church windows, my mother's dress, the cake, or the guests. Instead, the memory that twirls around in my head is the feeling of weightlessness I experienced as I nestled in his arms and we twirled around the dance floor, my sticky lollipop inches from his neatly combed hair.

Did I realize he was my new stepfather? At three years old, I don't think so. I didn't know the story about the first time he met my mom. I didn't know about their struggles to let go of the past and look toward a new future. I didn't know how he'd proposed or whether or not he was overwhelmed with the responsibilities of becoming an overnight parent to three little girls. And at that moment, I didn't care that my sisters were impatiently waiting for their turn or that I had stolen the groom from his bride. All I knew was that he was my daddy—and we were dancing.

A few years went by and Mom and Dad added another girl to the family, but this one was his by blood. Surprisingly it didn't alter my world at all, except for the fact that I couldn't pronounce her name! Dad never changed. He didn't brush us aside in a rush to the bassinet when he came home from work, and he didn't start calling us his stepdaughters now that he had a daughter of his very own. He'd always introduced us as "his girls" from the very beginning, and he kept right on doing it. Never once during all those years did I feel like a stepchild.

Our blended family had merged together so swiftly that years went by before it even dawned on me that I wasn't his. From the day they'd said "I do," he was saying "I will" to the three little girls in the first pew.

Several more years went by, and although the memories of that first dance faded, they were replaced with new ones. Dancing in the kitchen while Johnny Horton's mellow voice swirled around us in Western ballads, twirling and stomping to our favorite country artists and watching Mom's cheeks flush as he whispered in her ear while they swayed. Then we each got a turn to dance with him, and in his arms we felt loved, protected, and cherished. As I think back on those days, the word *stepfather* never enters my mind. All I recall is that he was my daddy—and we were dancing.[1]

The greatest happiness in life is the conviction that we are loved, loved for ourselves, or rather, loved in spite of ourselves.

VICTOR HUGO

Heavenly Father,

Thank You for providing the perfect example of what a father's love should be. You are a friend in whom I can always confide. You love me enough to say yes to those things that are good for me and no to those things You know are not in my best interest. Even when I fail, or when I choose to follow my own way, Your love for me remains the same. You love me enough to discipline me, knowing that I'll find my greatest contentment and fulfillment in living according to Your way.

Help me to follow Your example as a father. Give me the wisdom to know when my children need me to be their friend and when they need me to exercise the authority You've given me as their father. Teach me to love them in such a way that our relationship will point them to a personal relationship with You, their Heavenly Father.

Amen.

I THANK GOD for you,
my loving DAD!

You're the

BEST

DAD

in the World Because...

You Teach Me How
to Enjoy Life.

Some of the best things you can give

your children are good memories.

AUTHOR UNKNOWN

A cheerful heart is good medicine.

PROVERBS 17:22

You've just come home from a long day at work, and the only thing you want to do is lie down and rest. But you're greeted at the door by the eager smiles of children awaiting their much-anticipated playtime with Daddy. With a longing glance toward the sofa, you sweep a little one up in your arms, and the games are underway. You soon know you've made the right choice, for their smiles are contagious and, though you're still tired, your heart is much lighter, and the cares of the day don't seem to weigh on you quite so heavily.

With all the pressure to be and have the best, it's not easy to pull away from life's responsibilities and just enjoy time with your family. But it is so important. As the head of your household, you set the tone for your family. If you bring home stress, tension, and grumpiness, your children are likely to reflect these same attitudes. But if you approach your family with joyfulness, your home will become a haven of peacefulness and cheer where you can be refreshed for the days ahead.

A TRIBUTE TO MY DAD

Some of my best childhood memories are of ordinary moments that my dad made special. He's always loved all kinds of music, and he'd often play something on the stereo while he cleaned up the dinner dishes. Jazz was one of his favorites. My sisters and I would go in and start dancing to the music, and Dad would join us, swinging us around wildly and dancing his silliest dance. Then he'd grab Mom, and our kitchen-turned-ballroom would be filled with laughter, the whole family, including the dogs, joining in.

Going out to eat was a special treat because he'd take a deck of cards and we would play a game or he'd show us a card trick while we were waiting for the food. I'm grateful for the many special memories he's made for my sisters and me. It always seemed to come so naturally, but now that I'm older, I've come to appreciate how much effort he put into making every day fun for us.

A. J. MORIAH

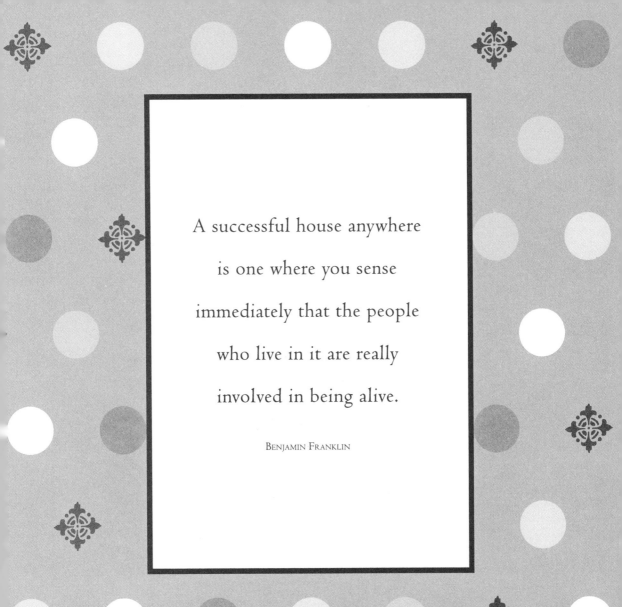

A successful house anywhere

is one where you sense

immediately that the people

who live in it are really

involved in being alive.

Happy fathers make happy children.

AUTHOR UNKNOWN

THE COUNTY FAIR

Georgia A. Hubley

As I ate breakfast, my excitement mounted as I stared at the date I'd circled on the calendar hanging on our farmhouse kitchen wall. I counted under my breath . . . "Only ten more days until the county fair!" I announced. "And this year I'm old enough to ride the Tilt-a-Whirl."

My parents glanced at one another and their smiles faded. Immediately I knew something was wrong. Dad frowned and his jaw tightened. "Honey, I'm afraid there's no money for the county fair this year. The drought has wiped out our corn crop."

For a moment I sat there dumbstruck. I swallowed hard and choked back the tears. "But you said when I was six, I could ride the Tilt-a-Whirl," I whined.

"I know you're disappointed, but I promise we'll go next year," Dad said.

I buried my face in my hands and began to cry. Then through my tears and hurried gulps of air, I stammered, "I wish I could have my own county fair."

"I think we can do just that," Dad said. "Follow me. We're going to make you a Tilt-a-Whirl."

I tagged along with Dad to the barn and watched him gather tools and salvage a four-foot wooden wagon wheel with a broken axle that was stored there. I skipped beside him as he rolled the wagon wheel to an old maple tree stump nearby.

I observed while Dad secured the wagon wheel at an angle, then anchored it into the soil below the tree stump. "There's your Tilt-a-Whirl. Give it a try," Dad said, grinning.

I climbed onto the wagon wheel and placed my feet in between two of the spokes at the bottom of the wheel. I clasped my hands on top of the wheel, placing my head on the spoke separating my hands. With a quick twist of my body from side to side, the wheel began to turn. The old wheel whirred as I went round and round. I didn't even get a bit dizzy! Indeed, I had my very own Tilt-a-Whirl. "Thank you, thank you!" I squealed, as I twirled around on the wagon wheel. "I'm going to make tickets and invite my friends to ride, too."

The following afternoon, several friends came to ride my wheel ride. Dad was the ticket taker and wheel ride operator. "Your dad is the best," one friend whispered. I had to agree, as I was blessed to have such a fun-loving, caring Dad.

As promised, Dad took me to the county fair the following year, and I had my first ride on the "real" Tilt-a-Whirl. Afterward, Dad asked, "Was it better than your wheel?"

"Yes," I replied, "but no one has a wheel like mine."[2]

You can do anything

with children if you only

play with them.

Be kind to thy father,

for when thou wert young,

who loved thee so fondly as he?

He caught the first accents

that fell from thy tongue;

and joined in thy innocent glee.

MARGARET COURTNEY

When a man dies, if he can pass enthusiasm along to
his children, he has left them an estate of incalculable value.

THOMAS EDISON

Heavenly Father,

So often, I get caught up in the responsibilities and pressures of work and forget to have fun and enjoy the family You've blessed me with. When I do that, I start to feel further away from being the person I want to be, the person You intended for me to be. By trying to please everyone, I end up letting down those who mean the very most to me.

Help me to strike the right balance between work and home. Renew my energy so I can give the time I have with my family the priority and effort it deserves. Give me creative ideas for making our time together meaningful and fun. Keep me ever mindful that the memories I create with my kids will far outlast anything I could buy for them with a bigger paycheck.

Amen.

I THANK GOD for you,

my fun-loving DAD!

You're the

BEST

DAD

in the World Because...

You're My

Greatest Fan.

Nothing has a better effect

upon children than praise.

SIR PHILIP SIDNEY

> I have great confidence in you; I take great pride in you.
> I am greatly encouraged.
>
> 2 CORINTHIANS 7:4

Do you let your children know how proud you are of them? Sometimes as parents we can become so concerned with correcting bad behavior in our children that we tend to focus on the negative in our interactions with them, rarely talking to them about what they do right.

Because sons naturally seek the approval of their fathers and daughters often gravitate toward men who respect them to the same level that their fathers do, it's vital to let your children know what it is you admire about them. When they bring home report cards, be sure you notice the good grades before talking about lower grades. Praise their successes at a sport or other activity they're interested in. And most important of all, point out moments when they display maturity, thoughtfulness toward others, and strength of character. Your affirming words will brighten their day and could change their tomorrow.

A LETTER TO MY DAD

Dear Dad,

You've always been easy to pick out of a crowd. You were the one cheering loudest at my games, the one wiping tears off your cheeks at my recitals, the one standing tallest and clapping hardest at award ceremonies. As I was growing up, there was one thing I knew without any doubt—my daddy was proud of me, and he loved me very much.

Though I'm not in front of crowds much anymore, some things haven't changed. I can still see the pride in your eyes as you play with your grandchildren. You cheer me on still, even in the small responsibilities of everyday life. When I get discouraged or feel like I've failed in some area, there's still one thing I know for sure—my daddy is proud of me, and he loves me very much. Thank you, Dad, for always being there to cheer me on.

Love,

Your Child

The praises and compliments

I received from my father

are worth more to me than

any others in the world.

CHARLOTTE MAE

Correction does much,

but encouragement does more.

JOHANN WOLFGANG VON GOETHE

SUN-KISSED

CAROL MCADOO REHME

My Celtic heritage evidenced itself in typical fashion: auburn hair, slate blue eyes, and fair skin. Freckles were a given. The dreaded dots spotted my legs, splashed my arms, speckled my face. And I despised them, each and every one, mostly because of the teasing that resulted.

After a particularly bad day in fourth grade, I flew into Daddy's arms.

"I h-hate them. I just hate them!"

"Your friends?"

"N-no, m-my *freckles.* I wish I could erase them!" My sobs grew louder as Daddy rubbed my back.

"You do? Why, that's silly, Torchie. I love your freckles," he said. "And one day you'll love them, too."

"Love them?"

"Love them," he promised. Daddy's work-rough hand smoothed back my matted bangs. "Those freckles simply show the places where you were kissed by the sun. See here?" His thick finger feathered the nutmeg sprinkles across my cheeks and nose. "One, two, three, four, five . . ."

My nose twitched at the tickles, and I giggled through my tears. Daddy nodded. "Yep. Kissed by the sun." He tweaked my nose. "From now on, you just tell everyone you were kissed by the sun. And tell them I said so."

So I followed Daddy's inspired advice and did exactly that. What began as an excuse soon became a boast. The words "my *daddy* says" slipped freely from my lips, giving me a growing sense of validation. I loved holding this coveted new center of attention, almost bragging about my freckles. Or at least until the fifth grade . . . when I got my first boyfriend.

"Where'd you get those freckles?" Jeffrey flicked the curl at the end of my brick-red braid one day. "They're kinda cute."

Although I blushed at the compliment, my answer by then was automatic; I tossed it out as casually as I smoothed my polished cotton skirt. "Oh, that's where I was kissed by the sun."

"Oh, yeah?" Jeffrey grabbed my arm masterfully, turned me to face him, and looked me in the eye. "And just *whose* son did the kissing?" he demanded.

"Uh . . . well . . . uh . . ." A deep blush crept up my neck and swept across my cheeks.

"Well, if he can," said Jeffrey, "so can I!"

Then, before I could explain, he leaned forward with a proprietary air and planted a firm kiss . . . squarely on my cheek. Wide-eyed, I cupped my face and watched Jeffrey's flush crimson.

Daddy was right, I decided then and there, I *loved* my freckles.[3]

It is a wise father that knows his own child.

WILLIAM SHAKESPEARE

Heavenly Father,

Thank You for blessing me with great kids. They do so many things that make me proud. Help me to know how to best express my admiration of each of them. Give me insight into the things they're passionate about; I want to understand those interests so I can encourage them and be involved in the areas of their lives that are important to them.

I want my kids to know that I'm always in their corner, whether they're winning or losing, through good times and bad. Help me to know when they need my words of encouragement and when they just need me to listen. And help me to notice and acknowledge all the good things they do, especially those related to displaying godly character.

Amen.

I THANK GOD for you, DAD.

You make me feel like I'm the greatest!

You're the

BEST

DAD

in the World Because...

You Inspire Me to
Do My Best.

To set a lofty example is the richest

bequest a man can leave behind him.

SAMUEL SMILES

> We continually remember before our God and Father your
> work produced by faith, your labor prompted by love, and your
> endurance inspired by hope in our Lord Jesus Christ.
>
> 1 Thessalonians 1:3

As a dad, you're often called upon to coach your children—not just in Little League but in life. They look to you for guidance, assurance, and encouragement.

The best coaches have a firm grasp on the fundamentals on which they want to build their team, and they work hard to get their team members on board with their ideals. They know their players must really believe in what they're doing in order to put forth their best effort.

Do you have a firm grasp on the fundamentals that you want to build your family on and do you communicate these fundamentals to your children? Do they understand the beliefs that motivate your actions? When your children are on board with your ideals, they'll be inspired to do their very best.

A TRIBUTE TO MY DAD

I've never seen my dad do anything halfheartedly. In his quiet way, he goes about a task with everything he has, never seeking the recognition of others, just satisfied with the results of a job well done. And he's never been afraid to tackle anything, from auto mechanics to creating a pattern for a sewing project I had in mind. If he didn't know how to do something, he'd read and learn about it until he found out.

When I brought projects home from school, he'd never let me settle for doing less than my best. Instead, he would spend hours helping me, stretching me beyond what I thought myself capable of.

My dad instilled in me a standard of excellence that has helped me greatly throughout the years, and he did it without a lecture, without stern discipline or cajoling. His quiet example was a great inspiration to me. Without it, I would probably never know just how much I could achieve.

SHAWNA MCMURRY

Love does not dominate;

it cultivates.

JOHANN WOLFGANG VON GOETHE

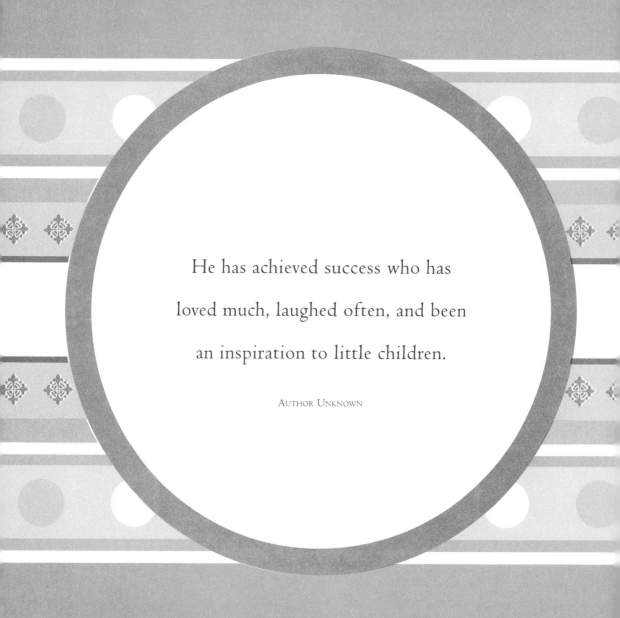

He has achieved success who has
loved much, laughed often, and been
an inspiration to little children.

AUTHOR UNKNOWN

THE BEST PART OF WAKING UP

CAROL McADOO REHME

I've never been a coffee drinker. Unless, of course, you count the sip I sneaked at age five.

Finally deemed old enough to fix and carry an insulated mug of Daddy's favorite brew, I stirred in a heaping teaspoon of sugar followed by a swirl of thick cream. I knew the exact measurement because I'd watched him do it countless times—add a splash of cream before twirling the mug between his work-roughened palms.

He made it look so desirable. Yet . . .

"Coffee isn't for little girls," he'd say when I begged. "It'll put hair on your chest."

Steadying the steaming cup between both chubby hands, I inched my way from the counter, careful not to slosh. Tendrils of fragrant Folgers teased my nose. Tempted by the milky-sweet scent, I actually did it: I took a quick sip.

Today, I recall the scald more than the taste. Even so, I still can't resist the smell of coffee. To me it's redolent of home; it spells D-a-d-d-y.

Every morning of my childhood, I woke to the sound and scent. Mother rose early to have the pot percolated by the time Daddy dressed for work. In later years, my gadget-minded father purchased the first timed coffee brewer to hit the market. After that, they took turns setting it so that they, too, awoke to the scent.

On our annual summer camping trips, Daddy let us all sleep late. In the crisp predawn, he flexed his arms and chopped wood, setting aside splinters for kindling. Before long, a fire flamed in the rock-ringed pit while a sooty coffeepot bubbled on its fringes. In a huge iron skillet, he crisped bacon and reserved the grease for a mess of hash browns. As he cracked eggs into the pan, he called us from the tent.

"Coffee's on!" he whisper-shouted.

He never announced breakfast itself—seasoned with pungent wood smoke—which he'd lovingly prepared for us all. A simple "Coffee's on!" urged us from the warmth to fill our plates by the fire.

"Coffee's on!" Those two words said it all.

The first time I brought home my husband-to-be, Daddy took him aside for a manly visit over a freshly brewed cup of coffee, a privilege I'd never been afforded. And, from across the kitchen, he looked at me, raised an eyebrow . . . and winked his reassuring approval.

My daddy died a few years back. When I traveled home to visit

Mother later, his absence in the house was heart-wrenching. One morning I spoke up.

"Everything feels different without Daddy. It even smells different."

I stared down into my glass of orange juice and frowned. "That's it!" I looked at Mother. "The smell of coffee! Why don't I smell coffee?"

She shook her head with a sad smile. "No need to brew a pot. I heat it in the microwave, one cupful at a time."

A sad state of affairs, for certain. But of course she was right. Still, the house no longer smelled like home.

Maybe that's why I burn coffee-scented candles in my own house. Why I sometimes accept a brimming mug to roll between my palms. It's an opportunity to inhale the memories, and a fragrant reminder to give of myself, to serve those I love, to be the best I can be in everything I do . . . just like Daddy did.

Still, I can't quite bring myself to drink the stuff. I don't want to risk getting hair on my chest![4]

When you thought I wasn't
looking, I saw you always did
your best, and it made me want
to be all that I could be.

AUTHOR UNKNOWN

A child's life is like a piece of paper on which

every passerby leaves a mark.

AUTHOR UNKNOWN

In praising or loving a child, we love and praise not that which is, but that which we hope for.

JOHANN WOLFGANG VON GOETHE

Heavenly Father,

My children look to me for approval, and I know that a large part of their self-worth is wrapped up in their idea of what I think of them. How do I let them know how proud I am of them just as they are, yet still motivate them to grow and improve? What should I require of them, and how do I know when my expectations are unrealistic?

As I think about these questions, Micah 6:8 comes to mind. It raises the question, "What does the LORD require of you?" The answer is, "To act justly and to love mercy and to walk humbly with your God." What You require of me as Your son is a great example of what I should require of my children. I don't think anything could make a father prouder than a child who does that—acts justly, loves mercy, and walks humbly with You.

Amen.

I THANK GOD for you,

my inspiring DAD!

You're the

BEST

DAD

in the World Because...

You Set a

Good Example.

What we desire our children to become,

we must endeavor to be before them.

ANDREW COMBE

In everything set them an example
by doing what is good.

TITUS 2:7

Whose example do you follow? Are there other men whom you look up to and go to for advice and mentoring? In 1 Corinthians 11:1, Paul exhorts the church at Corinth to "Follow my example, as I follow the example of Christ." Having someone you can look up to and emulate in certain areas can be a great help as you strive to be a person whom your children can look up to.

Of course, the best example you can follow is that of Christ Jesus. An excellent topic of study for your devotional time would be the characteristics and attributes of Christ. How can you apply the way Jesus handled situations He encountered to situations you find yourself in today? Which of His characteristics would help you to become a better father?

A LETTER TO MY DAD

Dear Dad,

From as early as I can remember, I can't name a time that you expected something of me that you didn't expect of yourself. In fact, you've always held yourself to a much higher standard than you hold others to. You taught me the importance of reading the Bible and praying each day, not only by encouraging me to do so, but by doing so yourself.

You taught me to be honest by dealing honestly with everyone yourself. You demonstrated to me how to honor others by always considering the needs of others before your own. You showed me how to repent and accept forgiveness by being honest about your shortcomings and readily asking forgiveness when you were wrong. Thank you, Dad, for giving me a firsthand example of what it means to be Christlike.

Love,

Your Child

You must be careful how

you walk, and where you go,

for there are those following

you who will set their feet

where yours are set.

ROBERT E. LEE

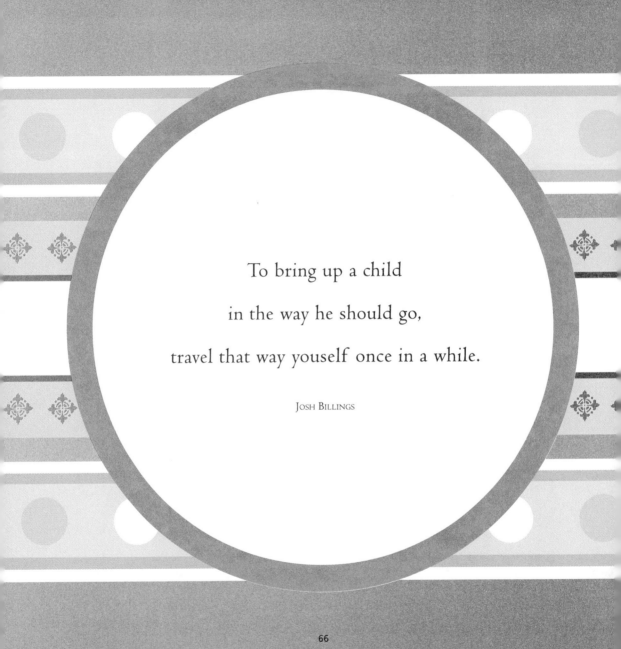

To bring up a child

in the way he should go,

travel that way youself once in a while.

JOSH BILLINGS

HIS INSPIRING MOTTO

RENIE BURGHARDT

I was ten when we fled our Soviet-occupied country Hungary, in 1947, landing in a refugee camp in Austria. Our only worldly possessions were the clothes on our backs. We had lost everything because of World War II, but we were alive, and for that we were grateful to God.

The refugee camp housed hundreds of destitute refugees. Although dismal and cramped, the camp provided a roof over our heads, donated clothes to wear, and soup and bread to fill our hungry stomachs. So what did it matter that we didn't have a penny to our names?

But it mattered a great deal to Apa (Hungarian for Dad). He hated living off the charity of others, hated not being able to provide for his family, as he always had in the past.

Just beyond our dismal camp home was a beautiful natural world of mountains, a crystal clear river, and farms with grazing animals. The river was the Drau River, and Apa and I discovered it on a summer day while taking one of our rambles through the countryside.

"You can enjoy the water while I get busy with something else," he said.

So I splashed around in the shallow, clear water while Apa walked up and down the bank. I noticed he was cutting some branches from the river willows growing all along the bank. Soon he had a large armful of them, so we headed back to camp.

"What are you going to do with them?" I asked him curiously.

"I will make some baskets," Apa replied.

"And what will you do with the baskets?" I asked, suddenly remembering that his hobby used to be weaving.

"I will try and sell them to the Austrians."

Soon Apa found some old boards and bricks and set up a worktable in front of our barrack. Then, after peeling the willow branches, he began weaving his first basket. A large crowd gathered to watch him. Some boys volunteered to get more willow branches for him.

"Thank you. And when I sell my baskets, I'll pay you for your help."

Within a short time, there were six beautiful baskets ready for the market. Apa hung them on a long stick, flung them over his shoulder, and off he went to town. He returned a few hours later minus the baskets. He had sold all of them!

Then he reached into his pocket and pulled out the book I had been longing for while we had walked around in town.

"Oh, thank you, Apa!" I shrieked, giving him a hug. "I can't believe you were able to buy me a new book!"

"You are welcome, sweetheart. Never forget—where there is a will, there is always a way," he said. Then he went off to pay the boys who had helped him.

Apa continued with his new venture all summer and even gave free lessons in weaving to anyone interested. After he sold the next batch, he bought himself a fishing pole, too, and a large frying pan. Then, building a fire outside the barrack, he soon cooked up a large batch of fish he caught in the river and shared it with our neighbors. It was most unusual to have the aroma of that frying fish wafting through the camp, where barracks were lined up like soldiers, and helpless people lived their lives in them, hoping and praying for something better.

My dear Apa's example was an inspiration to many at that refugee camp. His inspiring motto also became my motto in my own life, and it has always served me well.[5]

You yourself must be an
example to them by doing
good works of every kind.
Let everything you do
reflect the integrity and
seriousness of your teaching.

TITUS 2:7 NLT

Children learn to deal with adversity

and triumph when they observe

their fathers remaining calm in the face of one

and humble in the face of the other.

Author Unknown

A man's worth depends on whether he has taught his children integrity, through his own example.

Robert Browning

Heavenly Father,

Thank You for being the ultimate example of what a father should be. In Your Word, You've revealed everything I need to know in order to be the father my children need. As I study the Bible, help me to understand its relevance to my life and the situations I face as a father.

Because You are my Father, I know You understand everything I'm going through. You know what a blessing children are and the joy and pride children can bring to their father. You also know how it feels when Your children are disobedient. You understand the pain of watching them try to handle things in their own way when You know what would be best for them. Thank You for Your fatherly heart that gives me strength and encouragement for the joyous challenge before me.

Amen.

I THANK GOD for you, DAD.

You're a great example to follow!

You're the
BEST
DAD
in the World Because...

You Share
Your Wisdom and
Insights for Life.

A father who shares his heart with his child gains his child's heart in return.

EDGAR GANDOLF

> Listen, my son, accept what I say, and the years
> of your life will be many. I guide you in the way
> of wisdom and lead you along straight paths.
> When you walk, your steps will not be hampered;
> when you run, you will not stumble.
>
> PROVERBS 4:10–12

How do you respond when your children come to you with questions? Life gets busy, and the temptation is to come up with a quick answer so you can get back to what you were doing. But if you'll make a practice of taking the time to really focus and give a well-thought-out answer, the results will be well worth the extra time.

And there's no need to wait for your children to have questions. Maybe you learned something from a situation at work or read something that sparked a thought. Bring it up in conversation with your kids. They may or may not seem interested at the time, but you'll never know what they'll take hold of until you talk with them. And they'll appreciate the time and attention from you.

A LETTER TO MY DAD

Dear Dad,

When I was growing up, we'd sometimes take walks together. I remember loving those walks and the easy conversations that came with them. It was a great chance for me to ask all my "why" questions. "Why do leaves change colors? Why don't all birds fly? Why is grass green?" And you'd have an answer for every one.

Our conversations would often turn to God and the Bible, probably because He's always been such an integral part of your life and you would fit Him in naturally to most of your answers to my questions. You'd use scriptures that you'd committed to memory to answer some of my questions. I'll always cherish those walks with you, Dad, and the wisdom you shared along the way.

Love,

Your Child

When you teach your son,

you teach your son's son.

THE TALMUD

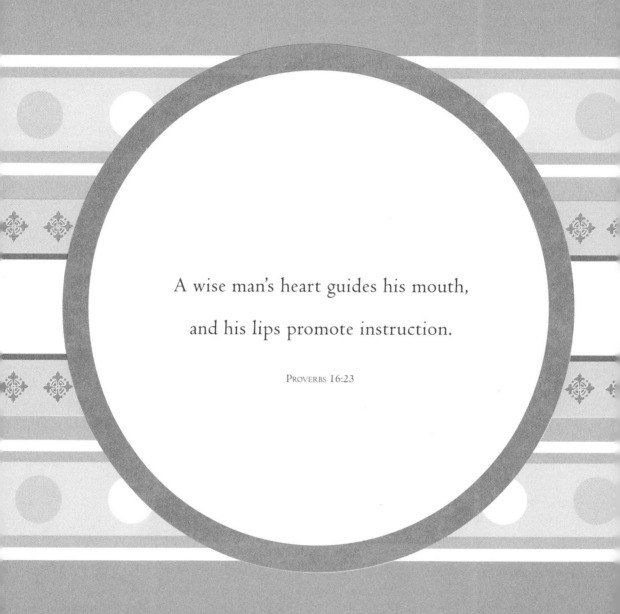

A wise man's heart guides his mouth,

and his lips promote instruction.

FROM DADDY'S YOUNGEST GIRL

NANCY SWIATEK PARDO

The OB nurse apologized to my father.

I was born in the era when dads were not allowed in the birthing room. So the nurse stepped into the fathers' waiting room to deliver what she apparently thought was less than good news. "I'm sorry, Mr. Swiatek, but you have *another* girl." I was his fourth daughter, the last hope for a son.

Never once in my life do I remember him saying, "If only you were a boy." He was a man ahead of his time. He always told my sisters and me, "You can be anything you want to be." One of his favorite phrases was "'Can't' means 'I don't want to.'"

My mother worked swing shift at a factory, so Dad was the one who tucked me in at night. Before bedtime, I would sometimes stand at the screen door, looking into the garage (which never held a car because it was his workshop), and watch him work the table saw. He was a master carpenter. Our home—turned from a one-bedroom cottage into a four-bedroom split-level—was a testament to his skill. He always smelled of sawdust and sweat; his hands were thick and rough and never came quite clean.

He never needed aid for spankings; his hands were tougher than any paddle. But those hands could painlessly remove the tiniest splinter from a foot, or tuck a blanket under a tired chin with gentle love. Those hands carried me, bleeding all over his white shirt, after I missed the baseball my sister pitched and it rearranged my nose.

He taught me how to pray the Lord's Prayer. He taught me if something's worthwhile, it's worth working hard for. Every good value I hold dear, I learned from him.

I miss him every time I need advice on how to fix something, or anytime I see a daughter with her dad at the market. I want to ask him so *many* things. "What did you see in the war, Dad? Why did you marry Mom? What was it about her that you loved so very much? What were your dreams, Dad? How did you get through losing your own parents so young?"

There's a disadvantage to being youngest—you get your parents for the least amount of time. And no matter how much time you have, it's never enough—enough to solve all the mysteries, enough to say, "I love you," enough to say, "I'm sorry," enough to ask, "May I sit in your lap just once more and feel your arms around me, your breath warm in my hair?"

How I *loved* being with him. He's been gone more than two decades, since just after my twenty-fourth birthday. Yet even now the smell of sawdust brings him vividly back to my heart, for I'm certain, even in Heaven, he still has sawdust in his trouser cuffs.

Thanks, Dad. For me, you were the best.[6]

These commandments that I give you today are to be upon your hearts. Impress them on your children. Talk about them when you sit at home and when you walk along the road, when you lie down and when you get up.

DEUTERONOMY 6:6–7

Heavenly Father,

You've revealed so much about Yourself and about the world around us in Your Word. You've laid out everything we need to know in order to live joyful, fulfilling lives that are pleasing to You. Help me to incorporate into my daily life the wisdom You've given me so my children will see the value of following Your instruction.

Remind me often of the importance of taking time to talk with my kids and to share with them the many lessons You've taught me along the way. As I strive to make the most of these valuable moments, I ask that You give me the right words to say at the appropriate time and that You open their hearts and minds to the lessons You would have them learn.

Amen.

I THANK GOD for you, DAD.

Your wisdom and guidance have shaped my life!

You're the

BEST

DAD

in the World Because...

You Give Me
Your Strength and
Encouragement.

A dad's encouragement can cause a

child to soar on wings of confidence.

ALEXANDER THORPE

> In repentance and rest is your salvation,
> in quietness and trust is your strength.
>
> ISAIAH 30:15

As a dad, you are relied upon to be the strength of the family, someone your children can always come to. But who do you go to when your strength is running low?

When great men in the Bible needed strength, they all went to the same source. The prophet Isaiah wrote, "Those who hope in the LORD will renew their strength" (Isaiah 40:31). David, who referred to God throughout the book of Psalms as his strength, said, "It is God who arms me with strength and makes my way perfect" (Psalm 18:32). When the apostle Paul cried out to God about his weakness, God responded, "My grace is sufficient for you, for my power is made perfect in weakness" (2 Corinthians 12:9).

Next time you need new strength to face the challenges of fatherhood, go to the Source of all strength, your Heavenly Father.

A LETTER TO MY DAD

Dear Dad,

I'm not sure anyone would really peg you for a "tough guy"; you've never been the type to throw your weight around to get your way. Yet when I hear the word strength, you're the first person who comes to my mind. You display an unwavering strength of character rarely seen today. You know exactly what you believe and why you believe it, and no amount of persuasion could cause you to waver from these beliefs.

With quiet humility, you command respect because of the level of excellence you hold yourself to. In your loving way, you encourage those around you to be their best just by being who you are. Thank you, Dad, for being a steady source of strength and encouragement and the type of person I can truly admire and seek to emulate.

Love,

Your Child

Encouragement is oxygen

to the soul.

GEORGE M. ADAMS

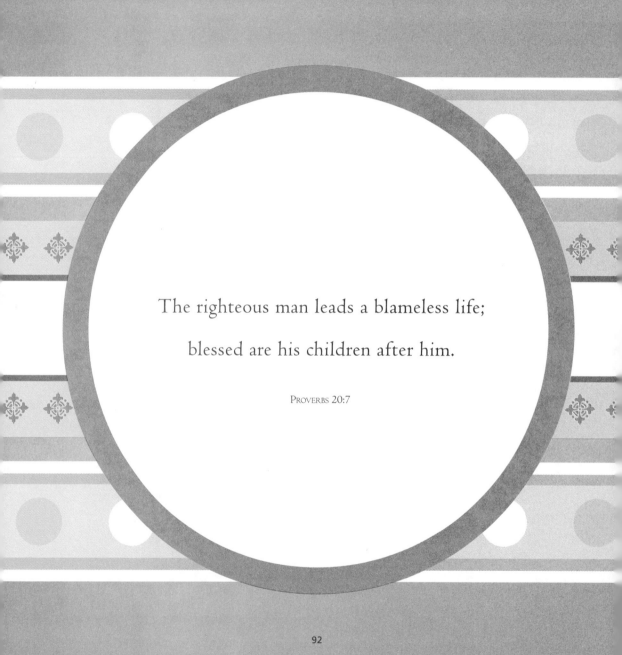

The righteous man leads a blameless life;

blessed are his children after him.

PROVERBS 20:7

THE STEPS OF MY FATHER

DONNA J. SHEPHERD

Luther Jack Riley, L.J. for short, was not a musical man. His wife, Mammie, grew up singing, and when they visited her family, the whole clan gathered around the piano to sing for hours. But not L.J.—he sat to the side and listened, never singing a note.

At the age of nine, Lavawan, the youngest of L.J. and Mammie's four children, found out his dad had a plan. Even though no one in the family had ever expressed a desire to play a musical instrument, for some inexplicable reason, his father decided to buy a piano. Lavawan could hardly sit still as L.J. told the family of the impending delivery.

Finally the day arrived. It rained hard that day, and the movers covered the wood with plastic sheeting. They rolled the old upright into the living room, and Lavawan's anticipation grew as they peeled back the plastic. He'd already begun calling it "my piano." He had such an unusual feeling about it all. He knew before he sat down he could play.

All four children took turns trying to play. One by one, they quit—except Lavawan. Every single day, he spent hours picking out notes. He had no teachers, no lessons, just a tenacious determination to learn.

L.J. worked shift work at the paper mill and often had to sleep during the day. It would be difficult for most people to sleep with a kid banging on the ivories for hours on end, but not L.J. Lavawan's mom pulled him aside to tell him she'd noticed something odd. "When you play the piano, your dad sleeps. When you quit, he wakes up."

One day Lavawan knelt down beside his bed and prayed a fervent prayer. "Please, God, if You'll give me the ability to play, I'll use it for Your glory the rest of my life." Within a few months' time, he could play almost every song the congregation sang at church. He became the church pianist at the age of ten.

Over the next few years, he learned to read and write music fluently. He became a concert pianist and played for thousands of people. Thousands more sang as he played in worship services. Lillenas Publishing Company has released several books of arrangements for piano by Lavawan Riley.

He testifies, "The call on my life depended on a decision and act of my father totally independent of me. He did not know I would become a pianist and serve in the ministry all these years. I know God guided my father's steps."

L.J. Riley passed away at the age of eighty-four. Lavawan played for his father's funeral. While he played, all he could think of was that day many years ago when his daddy felt led by the Holy Spirit to buy a piano.

As he filed past the casket, Lavawan laid his left hand on his father's lifeless right hand and prayed another fervent prayer. "God, these hands have finished their work. They toiled for years, and now they toil no more. But in my hands, there is still life, and I will use my hands to serve You the rest of my days. Thank You, God, for giving me such a father."[7]

Job description for dads: Must be loving, strong, and good at jokes.
Skills in ball throwing, hugging, and tickling a plus.
Must expect long hours; pay is all the love you can hold.

AUTHOR UNKNOWN

Heavenly Father,

I'm tired. Lately, I've fallen into a pattern of trying to do things in my own strength instead of relying on You. As a result, fatherhood, marriage, and my career have started to seem more like tasks than the wonderful God-given blessings that they are.

I don't like the job I do when I try to handle things without Your help. I come to You humbly, asking You to take over once again, to be my strength and to display Your power through my weakness. I place my trust in You, knowing that only through Your power working in me can I reach my full potential as a father, husband, employee, and any other role into which You've placed me. I rest in Your strength so that I can be a refuge for those who depend on me.

Amen.

I THANK GOD for you,

my strong and encouraging DAD!

You're the

BEST

DAD

in the World Because...

You Point the
Way to My
Heavenly Father.

As for me and my household,

we will serve the LORD.

JOSHUA 24:15

How great is the love the Father has lavished on us,
that we should be called children of God!

I JOHN 3:1

As a father, you are the first and most lasting impression your children will have of their Heavenly Father. It's an awesome responsibility, but also a great privilege. When you love your children without condition, you're showing them firsthand how the Father loves them. When you engage with them in conversation and listen attentively to their concerns, you're giving them a taste of how interested God is in having an intimate relationship with them. When you protect them from harm, you're demonstrating God's constant, watchful care over them. And when you discipline them, you're showing them how God demonstrates His love by correcting them when they go in a direction He knows will not be best for them.

As you go about the daily routine of fatherhood, keep in mind that you are a reflection to your children of the Father heart of God. You're doing the work of Heaven.

A LETTER TO MY DAD

Dear Dad,

God has never been an afterthought in our home or someone we talk about only on Sundays. When I was young, you read me Bible stories and prayed with me each night. When I learned to read, you made sure the Bible was one of the first books I practiced reading. And as I grew older, you encouraged me to spend time studying the Bible and praying on my own. It was always important to you that I form my own relationship with God and not rely on yours or Mom's. When I began to have questions about God's existence, you didn't condemn me for it; instead, you helped me work through those questions and find my own answers.

Thank you for leading me into a personal relationship with God through your constant commitment and your careful demonstration of His love.

Love,

Your Child

He who fears the LORD

has a secure fortress,

and for his children

it will be a refuge.

PROVERBS 14:26

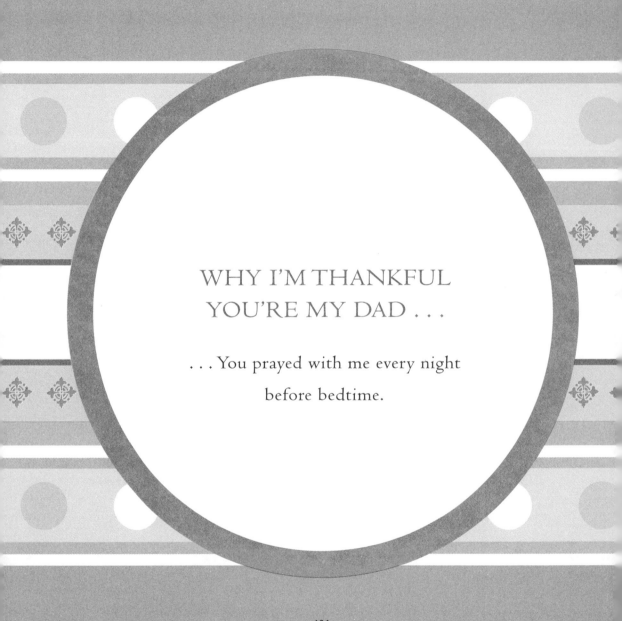

WHY I'M THANKFUL
YOU'RE MY DAD . . .

. . . You prayed with me every night

before bedtime.

OF WINGS AND STRINGS

CAROL MCADOO REHME

We children—grown and scattered to the four winds—had been reeled home to pick through the pieces of our beloved father's life. And, as familiar as a favorite cousin, the dusty ball of string was the treasure I snagged. I claimed it; I pocketed it—along with the memories it evoked.

Way back when, in an era before America was prepackaged and disposable, our family valued the virtue of thrift. Everyone saved something; we kids saved string. Twine from packages, whatever bits we could salvage and tie to our burgeoning balls. String had its uses: fashioning macaroni into necklaces, pulling a loose tooth, finger-weaving Cat's Cradle.

Mostly, though, we used it for kites.

Mother flattened and ironed crinkled Christmas paper that we spliced crazy-quilt style onto wooden sticks scrounged from Daddy's garage. We pawed through a cache of rags to add for wispy tails. And, knotting our string-balls to the diamond-frame contraptions, we answered the siren call of April winds.

But I trailed the others, slowed by the firm knowledge that mine wouldn't fly. No matter how brisk the breeze, my kite dogged my feet like a temperamental toddler. It waddled across the grass and usually rose with my hopes before it flapped, fluttered, and flopped to its back like a wounded goose.

One day Daddy laid his large workman's hand on my shoulder. "You need to give it more line," he explained.

"It still won't work. It never does."

"Just let it find its way." He turned his tanned face into the quickening breeze. "Run!" he shouted, grabbing the string above my clenched fist and racing with me into the wind as my cotton play-dress flattened against my thighs. "Okay, give it some slack . . . now!"

In spite of the kite's insistent tug, I held back. "What if it breaks away? I don't want to lose it."

"Now!" he repeated.

As I reeled out the string, the kite caught an air current, staggered, and nosed its way upward, winging toward freedom.

"It's flying!" I flashed a wide grin at the sky.

"Hold on firmly, but loosen the line some," Daddy ordered.

As I eased out the string, I felt the kite's heart thrum an erratic beat down the taut length. My heart echoed the rhythm. Farther and farther it flew, hesitating once to glance over its shoulder almost asking permission to continue. Sipping a first taste of liberty, it dipped and bobbed and whirled, dancing to the strains of music I felt but couldn't hear.

I turned to Daddy. "What holds it up?"

"Why, you"—he shrugged—". . . and the string."

"Oh, Daddy, that's silly. The string holds it down, not up."

"Look over there." He pointed at a tree whose branches impaled the bleached bones of a kite. "That's what happens when you let go of the string. The kite flies away but eventually it falls, see? The thing that anchors it lets it soar."

So the string really did keep the kite up even while holding it down. And that oddity made sense to me, the young child. The very things that anchor us actually let us soar.

The values, virtues, and lessons Daddy taught gave us the freedom to live virtuous lives . . . while tying us to heaven and home. And through Daddy's example, he showed us the love that our Heavenly Father has for us—the real anchor in my life that allows me to soar.

Yes, I caressed the raggedy ball of string nestled deep in my pocket. *This is the heirloom I'll treasure.* And I looped the loose end around my pinky, just as a reminder.[8]

Home is the seminary of all

other institutions.

A minister once asked a group of

children in a Sunday school class,

"Why do you love God?"

He got a variety of answers,

but the one he liked best was from

a little girl who said,

"I guess it just runs in the family!"

AUTHOR UNKNOWN

Keep yourself clean and bright—
you are the window through which your children see God.

Author Unknown

Heavenly Father,

More than anything else I could wish for them, I want each of my children to have a loving, personal relationship with You. I know that only in such a relationship will they be truly happy and find the fulfillment we all desire. Help me to know how to lead them toward You. I understand the decision must ultimately be theirs, but help me do what I can do to prepare them to make that choice.

Keep me ever mindful of the example I'm setting for them in the decisions I make in my own life. As I continue to seek You with all my heart, may they be encouraged to do the same. Help me to recognize and seize every opportunity to talk to them about You. May Your love shine through me toward them and may they be drawn to You.

Amen.

I THANK GOD for you, DAD.

You help me see how much God loves me!

You're the

BEST
DAD

in the World Because...

You Encourage
Me to Pursue My
Dreams.

A father's love and support are the

stepping stones for his child's future.

JOHN PRESCOTT

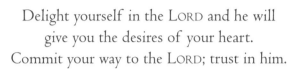

Delight yourself in the LORD and he will
give you the desires of your heart.
Commit your way to the LORD; trust in him.

PSALM 37:4–5

What are your children interested in? Do they show exceptional interest or ability in a certain area? Or maybe they are still searching for the niche that fits them best. As much as you're able, help them to explore many different avenues of interest. Expose them to the fine arts. Encourage them to participate in various sports. Take them to museums and encourage them to read books that may ignite an interest in certain areas of study. Once they latch on to a specific interest, stand behind them with your enthusiasm and support.

Pray with your children about their dreams and their plans for the future, and encourage them to follow God's leading. He has great plans for them, and He wants to work through you to help lead them into those plans.

A TRIBUTE TO MY DAD

My dad has always encouraged me to dream big. It was never important to him that I be interested in the most lucrative or the safest career path. Instead he instructed me to follow my passion because he knew that God placed those passions within me for a reason. He told me that it's in those things I'm most passionate about that I'll find my destiny, God's will for my life.

Through his example, my dad also showed me that my dreams won't necessarily be wrapped up in the way I earn my living. He's worked hard to support our family, and he has performed his work with excellence. But he also held on to the passion that God placed in his heart to write, blessing us and many others with the handiwork of his dreams. And his passion for being an excellent dad and husband has always been obvious to anyone who's known him. I'm so thankful for a dad who inspires and supports my dreams.

JADAELYN ANNALIESE

One of the greatest things

that a father can do for his

children is to encourage them

to discover their unique,

God-given gifts and pursue

their God-inspired dreams.

ANONYMOUS

A great father doesn't dream *for* his children, he encourages them to dream for themselves.

PAUL MEDLEY

WHY I'M THANKFUL
YOU'RE MY DAD . . .

. . . You always knew I would make

the world's best astronaut . . .

or dinosaur-hunter . . .

or veterinarian . . . or movie star . . .

or superhero!

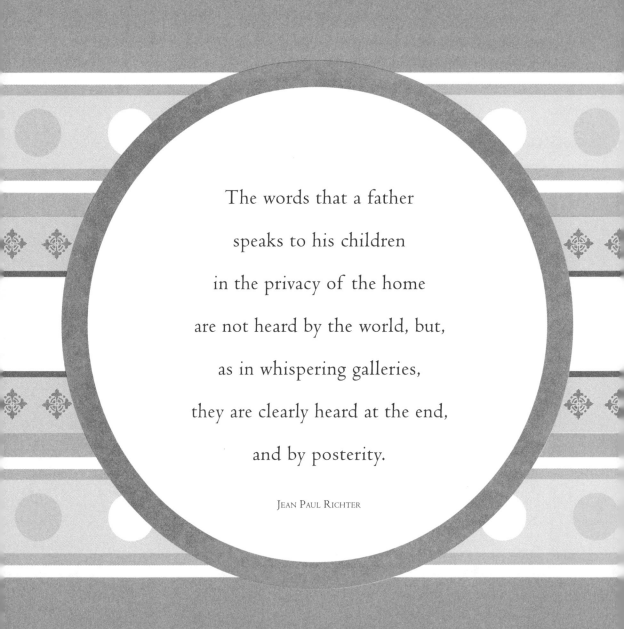

The words that a father

speaks to his children

in the privacy of the home

are not heard by the world, but,

as in whispering galleries,

they are clearly heard at the end,

and by posterity.

JEAN PAUL RICHTER

MY DAD, THE DREAMER

JULIE MORRISON

Looking out second-story windows we saw city sunsets cut through with telephone wires and pierced by electric poles. Exhaust fumes hung heavy in the air, except in those first few moments after a rainstorm. My dad is a dreamer.

"We'll have a house in the country one day with fresh air and a big wide-open sky. Every night sunsets will be painted all the way across as far as we can see," my dad said. In my eight-year-old mind, God's watercolors washed across the heavens. How could my dad see beyond now into the future? I saw swatches of firmament between tall brick buildings and neatly rowed two-story houses. I didn't see our new house in the country.

The summer after I turned ten, Dad bought a piece of country land with a real dirt road alongside. We stood atop our knoll, surrounded by five acres of goldenrod, milkweed, and thistles. Facing west, we watched the sun dip behind the maple woods. When the colors began to rainbow across the clear expanse, he winked at me. That moment, a dream became real.

"The front window of our new house will face the sunsets

and we'll watch them every night," he said, unwrapping another dream for me. "One day we'll leave our three-bedroom walk-up and live in a four-bedroom ranch-style home with a family room."

Before I started the sixth grade, we moved into our new, not-quite-finished house. Aside from the appliances and a cold-water sink, the kitchen hadn't been constructed.

"All you kids will get to help me build the kitchen," Dad said. "When it's done we'll have a big banana-split party and you can each invite a friend." For two years he made mounds of oak sawdust. He mopped up small white puddles of hide glue after clamping precision-cut pieces of wood together, making all the cabinets, doors, and drawers. We kids sanded miles of board feet and rubbed off the fine grit from reams of sandpaper, making sharp edges soft. When we finished our project, an eat-in bar stood between the kitchen and the dining room with honey-stained solid-wood cabinets above and below on all four walls. I was fifteen.

Just as I had dreamed, friends came over for a banana-split

party. My dad scooped everybody's choice of flavors into banana-lined bowls. We topped ice-cream balls with caramel, strawberry syrup, and chocolate sauce. All afternoon my dad practically glowed with pride in that kitchen. Our friends saw the sunset through the front windows of our new house.

"I want to accomplish so many projects," Dad said. "I'll have to live to be a hundred and twenty to get them all finished." Just like that, another dream planted itself in my head, where it lived until I turned forty-two.

Then Dad had a heart attack. Because of complications, the doctors didn't expect him to live through the night. I drove a hundred miles to stand by his ICU bed. I tried to think of something to hold his unconscious body to this side of heaven.

"I always dreamed you'd live to be a hundred and twenty. You still have fifty-one years left," I said. He kept right on living. Four years later, my dad is still a dreamer. Because of him, I am, too.[9]

Encourage one another and build each other up,
just as in fact you are doing.

I THESSALONIANS 5:11

Heavenly Father,

Thank You for inspiring dreams within my heart and the hearts of my children. When You have something specific You want us to do, You plant a desire deep within us to do that very thing. I know You have a special plan for each of my children. You've equipped them with talents that make them uniquely qualified for the tasks You've set before them.

As they grow in their relationships with You, I ask that You reveal to them in Your perfect timing Your plans for their lives. Give me the wisdom to know how to encourage them in that direction. Use me in any way You see fit to help equip them toward that end. May each of my children find their happiness in serving You with the abilities and desires You've given them.

Amen.

I THANK GOD for you, DAD.

You encourage me to reach for the stars!

There is something ultimate

in a father's love,

something that cannot fail,

something to be believed

against the whole world.

FREDERICK WILLIAM FABER

REMEMBER ME

SALLY CLARK

Daddy's handkerchiefs
lined his pockets with
embroidered linen;
dime-store packages of three
in shades of blue or gray or tan;
gifts from me
at Father's Day, Christmas,
and birthdays.

Faithfully prepared,
he was never without
the means or the desire
to catch my tears
and carry them home
to remember
at the end of the day
how he had been there
when I needed him.
Now my life is stocked
with white paper tissues
to blow my sorrows into
and easily dispose of
the evidence of my distress
into conveniently lined receptacles
strategically placed
throughout my life.

But in my pocket,
I still carry a
faded cotton memory of
his smooth-skinned care for me
and I will never forget
how he saved my tears
to remember me.[10]

NOTES

1. Paula J. Miller, Olivia, MN. Story used by permission of the author.
2. Georgia A. Hubley, Henderson, NV. Story used by permission of the author.
3. Carol McAdoo Rehme, Loveland, CO. Story used by permission of the author.
4. Ibid.
5. Renie Burghardt, Doniphan, MO. Story used by permission of the author.
6. Nancy Swiatek Pardo, Mount Prospect, IL. Story used by permission of the author.
7. Donna J. Shepherd, Middletown, OH. Story used by permission of the author.
8. Carol McAdoo Rehme, Loveland, CO. Story used by permission of the author.
9. Julie Morrison, Sunbury, OH. Story used by permission of the author.
10. Sally Clark, Fredericksburg, TX. Poem used by permission of the author.

LOOK FOR THESE BOOKS:

THE BEST FRIEND
IN THE WORLD

THE BEST GRANDMA
IN THE WORLD

THE BEST MOM
IN THE WORLD

THE BEST SISTER
IN THE WORLD

HOWARD BOOKS
A DIVISION OF SIMON & SCHUSTER
New York   London   Toronto   Sydney

THE BEST TEACHER
IN THE WORLD